SCHOLASTIC

20 Super Spelling Centers

Erica Bohrer

NEW YORK • TORONTO • LONDON • AUCKLAND • SYDNEY
MEXICO CITY • NEW DELHI • HONG KONG • BUENOS AIRES

Teaching *Resources*

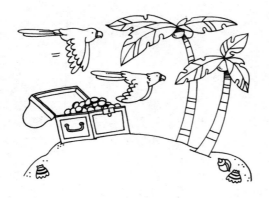

This book is dedicated to all of my fellow teachers and followers at
www.ericabohrer.blogspot.com (your supportive feedback is greatly appreciated),
and to three wonderful editors with whom I have had the pleasure of working,
Joan Novelli, Deborah Schecter, and Liza Charlesworth.

Cover design by Jason Robinson
Interior design by Kathy Massaro
Illustrations by Maxie Chambliss and Rusty Fletcher

ISBN: 978-0-545-37489-7

5   6   7   8   9   10   40   19   18   17   16   15   14   13

Contents

Spelling Centers

About This Book

20 *Super Spelling Centers* features ready-to-go, classroom-tested centers that motivate children to master the words on their spelling lists. The centers feature multisensory activities that work with any spelling-word list and can easily be reused with new words.

The best way for students to learn how to spell has long been a subject of debate, with the majority of research pointing to a systematic approach to teaching spelling (Schlagel, 2002). These findings suggest that direct spelling instruction is needed to give students the foundation they need for the spelling and reading of English words. Systematic strategies include rote memorization (drill and practice) and word study, an approach that invites students to explore patterns in words that they can then generalize to read and spell new words. *20 Super Spelling Centers* supports both approaches, offering opportunities to learn and reinforce spelling skills by spelling out loud, practicing writing the words, searching for words that share the same spelling pattern, and more. The activities are high-interest and often incorporate games and teamwork, providing students with both fun and effective ways to develop spelling skills.

The center activities in this book are designed to supplement your literacy program, and are perfect for use in the small-group setting of literacy centers. These activities however are not limited to small-group use; they are also suitable for whole-class and individual work, and may be used as homework activities to support spelling instruction outside of the classroom. You can use the spelling centers in any order that works best for you and your learners, and as many times as you like. In fact, I recommend using the same center activity for a few weeks in a row, varying the spelling words. Plan on about 20–30 minutes for students to complete each center.

Following is an overview of the features you'll find with each center.

* **List of Materials:** A convenient list of reproducible pages and any other materials necessary for the center is provided for quick reference.

* **Set Up the Center:** Each spelling center comes with a set of setup instructions, including helpful hints for modeling the center and supporting students' success.

* **Extend Learning:** An extension activity for each center provides further practice, with games, writing connections, partner quizzes, and more.

* **Directions:** Refer to the student directions page to explain and model each center activity. Place a laminated copy of this page at the center as a guide for other adults who may be working with students (i.e., classroom aides, parent helpers, substitute teachers).

* **Reproducible Pages:** Each center has two or three reproducible pages, such as pattern pages, word cards, and record sheets. Use the record sheets to help reinforce literacy skills and hold students accountable for their work in the center.

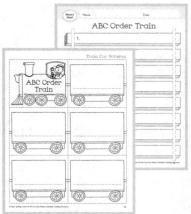

Getting Started

Research shows that expectations need to be modeled and practiced (Wong & Wong, 2004). In order for centers to run smoothly, students must know what is expected of them both behaviorally and academically. Teaching a set of procedures for materials use and "housekeeping" will lead to successful independent center time. The following guidelines provide a framework for modeling the use of any of the spelling centers in this book. In advance of modeling a center, enlarge reproducible pages so that all students can easily see them (for example, by creating a transparency for use with an overhead projector or by scanning to create an interactive whiteboard page). Depending on the center, you may also want to provide each student with a copy of the corresponding record sheet.

Lesson Guidelines

1. Review your list of spelling words with the class. (These centers work best with 5–10 spelling words.) Have students echo the words and the spelling of each one. (See Choosing Spelling Words, page 6.)

2. Introduce the spelling center and the materials students will use. Show students where to get the materials they will need.

3. Model the activity and guide students in helping you complete it (or a portion of it). Show students how to clean up and where to return the materials.

4. Together with children, brainstorm rules and expectations for the specific center. For example, with Stamp a Word (page 15), children may suggest that they should stamp their letters on the paper, stamp out extra ink on scrap paper before returning the stamp to the box, and wash their hands when they are finished.

5. Using a "gradual release of responsibility" approach, include the center as an independent literacy center choice once students understand the expectations.

Helpful Hints for Success

The spelling centers in this book require minimal preparation, but making sure that everything students need is in place will support success. Small plastic storage bins are a neat and portable way to house all the necessary materials for a spelling center. Depending on the center, you may want to keep a small wastebasket nearby for easy cleanup. Clearly label the bins and supplies. Make sure students know where to get the center bins and where to return them. It's important to review this routine before students begin work at a center. Other helpful hints follow.

* Keep students accountable for their center work by periodically walking around while centers are in progress. In order to have enough time to observe students in their center groups, I allow my centers to run for 30 minutes and limit my guided-reading group to 20–25 minutes.

* Announce when only five minutes remain before cleanup.

* Minimize interruptions by designating a "Center Captain" for each center. This student is responsible for being the "expert" at the center.

* Display a poster that reminds students of the things they can do if they finish their centers early.

* Reward center groups that have worked well. I staple a rewards chart under each group on the centerboard. After every rotation, I determine whether the group earned a "Center Star." This is simply a star sticker on the reward chart. When a group earns five stars, students may choose a prize from the "prize box" I keep in the classroom.

* Reward individual students for trying their best. I give students a special ticket if they have used center time productively. Five tickets earns a prize from the prize box. If a student has done exemplary work at a center, that work is displayed on the "Exemplary Center Work" clothesline. This student is responsible for being the "expert" at the center.

* At the end of center rotations, I invite students to share a piece of work with the class. All students are encouraged to share positive comments on their classmates' work.

Extension Activities

Consider the following suggestions to extend student learning with any of the centers.

✳ **A Colorful Classroom Display:** Children can bring their own creative touches to their record sheets by coloring the pages and adding details. Arranged on a bulletin board or other wall space, these record sheets make a colorful display that celebrates children's learning.

✳ **Word Work:** Many of the record sheets can help students see phonetic connections among their spelling words. Students can create a list of additional words following the same phonetic rules. For example, Sail Away With Vowels and Consonants (page 57) focuses attention on individual letters of a word. To extend learning, students can list words that share the same vowel, the same beginning or ending consonant, and so on.

✳ **Support Oral Language:** Encourage children to use their spelling words in sentences, stories, and riddles that they share orally with a partner. Example: "I'm thinking of a word that has [number] letters and begins with [letter]. What is it?"

Choosing Spelling Words

The composition of your spelling-word lists and the number of words you choose is up to you. I give my first graders 10 spelling words a week. These spelling words typically include five sight words with the same initial sound and five words that can be encoded using a spelling pattern, such as words with the same word ending. Whatever reasoning behind your spelling list, the centers in this book will support *your* list and provide an appealing and effective staple for your weekly literacy center rotations.

Connections to the Common Core State Standards

The spelling center activities in this book are designed to help you meet both your specific state English Language Arts standards as well as those recommended by the Common Core State Standards Initiative (CCSSI). These materials address the following standards for students in grades K–2. For more information, visit the CCSSI Web site: www.corestandards.org.

Reading: Foundational Skills

- Demonstrate understanding of the organization and features of print.
- Demonstrate understanding of spoken words, syllables, and sounds.
- Know and apply grade-level phonics and word analysis skills.

Language

- Demonstrate command of the conventions of standard English grammar and usage when writing or speaking.
- Demonstrate command of the conventions of standard English capitalization, punctuation, and spelling when writing.

References

Schlagel, B., (2002). Classroom spelling instruction: History, research, and practice. *Reading Research and Instruction.* 42(1), 44–57.

Wong, H. K. & Wong, R. T. (2004). *The first days of school: How to be an effective teacher.* Mountain View, CA: Harry K. Wong Publications.

Fishing for Spelling Words

Students go "fishing" for spelling words, then practice writing them to fill a fishbowl Record Sheet.

Set Up the Center

1. Laminate a copy of the Directions, and copy a class set of Record Sheets. If you have more than five spelling words, make extra copies of the Record Sheet.

2. Copy and cut apart the Fish Patterns. Write a spelling word on each fish, then color the fish and place them in the fish bowl.

3. Create and display an exemplary Record Sheet for students to use as a model.

4. Model the center work for students, making sure to point out that each word is written on a different fish. Remind students to return each fish to the fish bowl when they are finished writing the word. Show students that if you "catch a fish" for the second time, you place it back in the bowl and keep fishing until you catch a new fish.

Materials

- Directions (page 8)
- Record Sheet (page 9)
- Fish Patterns (page 10)
- Fishbowl (clear plastic container)

Extend Learning

When students have completed the activity, invite them to remove all of the fish from the bowl and place them facedown on the table. Students can take turns selecting a fish, reading and spelling the word, then returning the fish to the bowl.

Fishing for Spelling Words

Directions

1. Take a fish from the fishbowl.

2. Read the word on the fish.

3. Write the word on your Record Sheet.

4. Place the fish back in the fishbowl.

5. Repeat steps 1–4 to complete your Record Sheet. If you "catch a fish" for the second time, place it back in the bowl and keep fishing until you catch a new fish.

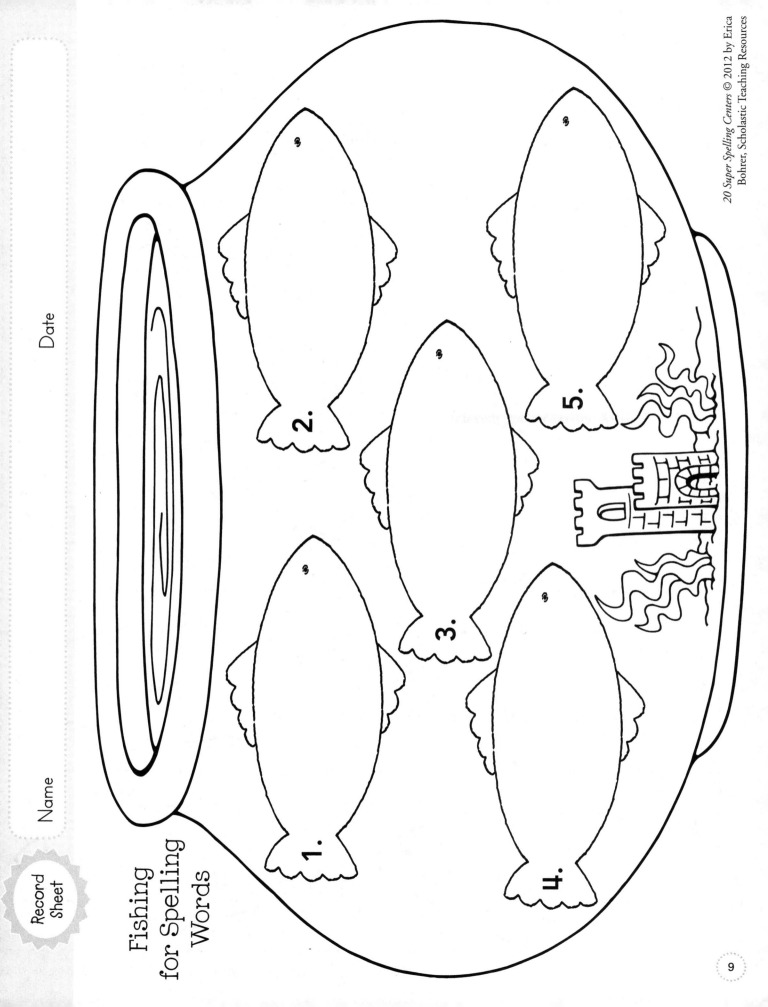

Record Sheet

Fishing for Spelling Words

Name

Date

Fish Patterns

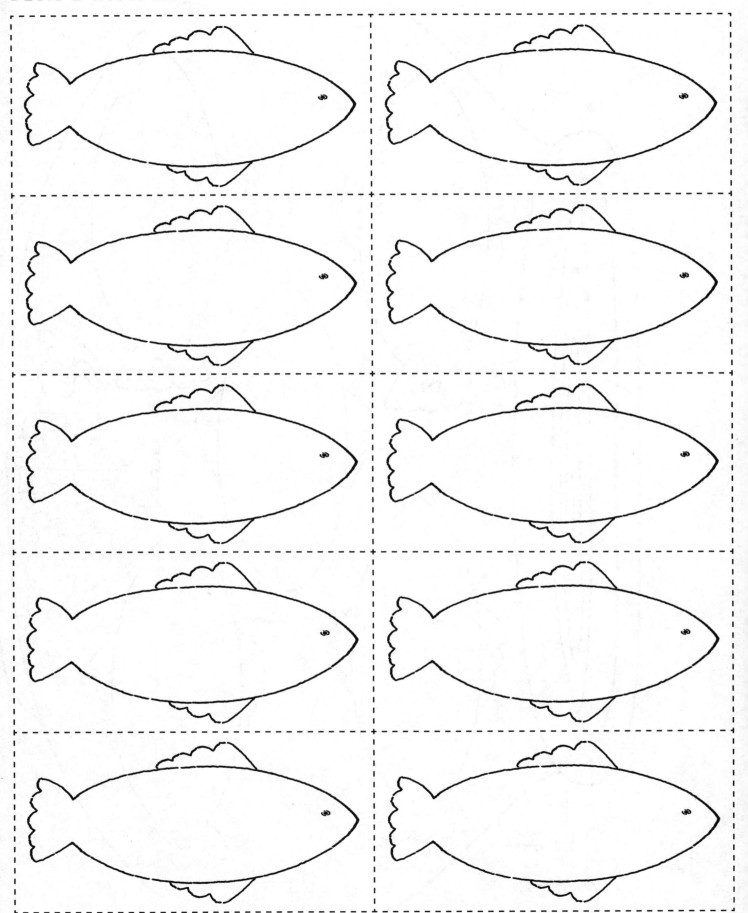

Brown Bag It

Students brown bag their spelling words by writing them on lunch-themed graphics. Then they pack up their words in a paper lunch bag—perfect for taking home to practice with families.

Set Up the Center

1. Laminate a copy of the Directions, and copy a class set of Record Sheets and Lunch Patterns.

2. Display the spelling words for the week (for example, on chart paper).

3. Create and display an exemplary Record Sheet for students to use as a model.

4. Model the center work for students, making sure to point out that they must write each spelling word on a different lunch pattern.

Materials

- Directions (page 12)
- Record Sheet (page 13)
- Lunch Patterns (page 14)
- Brown paper lunch bags

Extend Learning

When students have completed the activity, invite them to quiz each other on their spelling words. Have them take turns pulling out and reading one spelling word from their lunch bag for their partner to spell.

Brown Bag It

Directions

1. Read the list of spelling words.

2. Write each spelling word on a Lunch Pattern.

3. Color and cut out the Lunch Patterns.

4. Place the Lunch Patterns in a brown bag.

5. Pull out a Lunch Pattern from your bag.
   Write the word on your Record Sheet.

6. Repeat step 5 to complete your Record Sheet.
   Then put your Lunch Patterns back in the bag.

20 Super Spelling Centers © 2012 by Erica Bohrer, Scholastic Teaching Resources

Name

Date

Brown Bag It

1. _____

2. _____

3. _____

4. _____

5. _____

6. _____

7. _____

8. _____

9. _____

10. _____

Lunch Patterns

  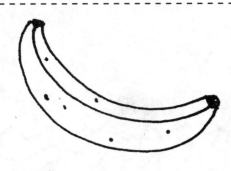

_____ _____ _____

_____ _____

_____ _____ _____

_____ _____

Stamp a Word

Students use alphabet stamps to practice spelling their words on grid paper.

Set Up the Center

1. Laminate a copy of the Directions, and copy a class set of Record Sheets. Note that this Record Sheet accommodates words of up to six letters. If the spelling words are longer than six words, tape two Record Sheets together to create space for longer words or use the Record Sheet as a model for creating one that works with longer words.

2. Display the spelling words for the week (for example, on chart paper).

3. Create and display an exemplary Record Sheet for students to use as a model.

4. Model the center work for students, making sure to instruct them to take one stamp at a time and to stamp one letter per box. You may want to show students how to remove excess ink from a stamp by pressing it on scrap paper before returning it to its case.

Materials

- Directions (page 16)
- Record Sheet (page 17)
- Alphabet stamps
- Washable ink (nontoxic)
- Scrap paper (optional)

Extend Learning

When students have completed the activity, invite them to stamp out a sentence on the back of their paper using one or more of the spelling words.

Stamp a Word

PUPPY
HUG
APPLE

Directions

1. Read the list of spelling words.

2. Stamp the first spelling word on your Record Sheet. Stamp one letter in each box.

3. Repeat step 2 to stamp out all your spelling words.

20 Super Spelling Centers © 2012 by Erica Bohrer, Scholastic Teaching Resources

Name   Date

 Stamp a Word

1					
2					
3					
4					
5					
6					
7					
8					
9					
10					

Chicks and Eggs

Students "crack" open colorful plastic eggs to find chicks with their spelling words, then practice writing the words in matching colors to reinforce color-recognition skills in the process.

Set Up the Center

1. Laminate a copy of the Directions, and copy a class set of Record Sheets.

2. Copy and cut apart the Word Card Patterns. Use the colored pencils to write a spelling word on each chick. (Write each word in a different color to match the eggs.) Place each chick inside an egg that is the same color.

3. Line the basket "nest" with paper "grass," and arrange the eggs inside.

4. Create and display an exemplary Record Sheet for students to use as a model.

5. Model the center work for students, being sure to point out that each word is written in the same color as its egg, and that students will use the same color pencil to write the word on their Record Sheet. Remind students to place the chick back inside the egg when they are finished writing the word, and then return the egg to the basket.

Materials

- Directions (page 19)
- Record Sheet (page 20)
- Word Card Patterns (page 21)
- Colored pencils (to match the egg colors)
- 10 large plastic eggs (assorted colors)
- Basket (without handles, for a "nest")
- Paper "grass" (shredded brown or green paper works well)

Extend Learning

When students have completed the activity, invite them to remove all of the chicks from the eggs and place them facedown on the table. Students can take turns selecting a chick, reading and spelling the word, and then returning the chick to its matching egg. Encourage students to help one another read the words as needed.

20 Super Spelling Centers © 2012 by Erica Bohrer, Scholastic Teaching Resources

Chicks and Eggs

Directions

1. Choose an egg from the nest.

2. "Crack" open the egg.
   Read the word on the chick.

3. Write the word on your Record Sheet.
   Use a pencil that is the same color as the egg.

4. Place the chick back inside the egg.
   Return the egg to the nest.

5. Repeat steps 1–4 for each egg in the nest.

Record
Sheet

Name

Date

Chicks and Eggs

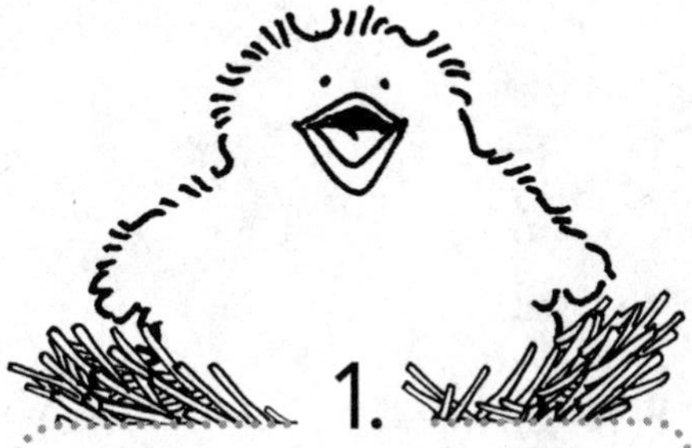

1.

2.

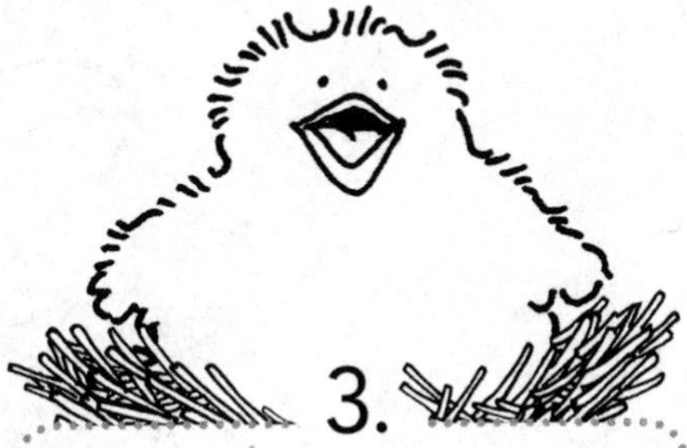

3.

4.

5.

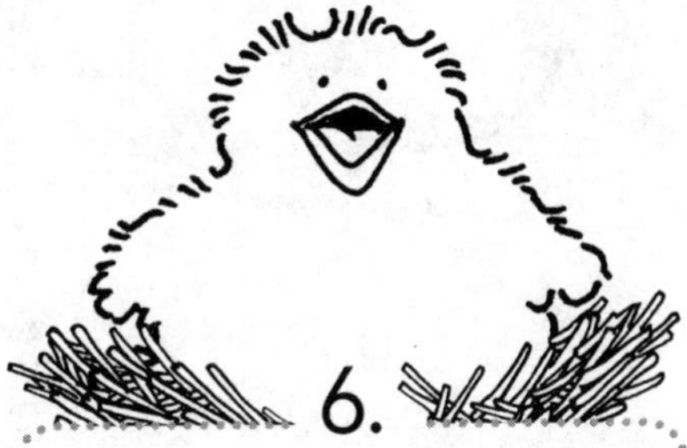

6.

7.

8.

9.

10.

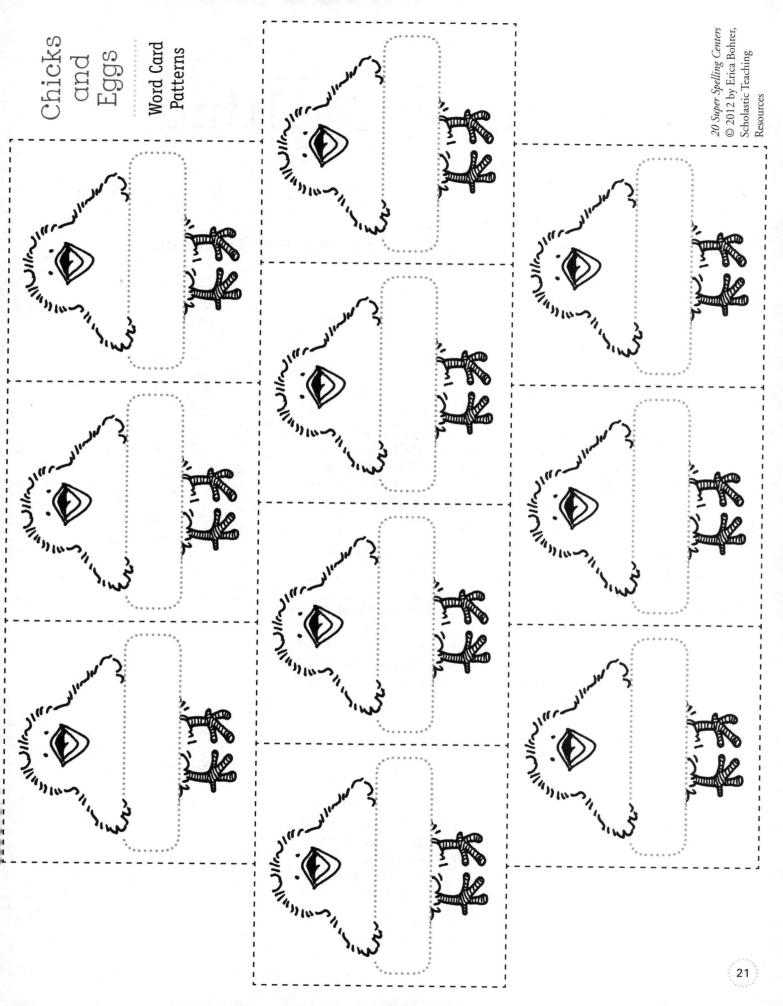

Chicks
and
Eggs

Word Card
Patterns

20 Super Spelling Centers
© 2012 by Erica Bohrer,
Scholastic Teaching
Resources

Rainbow Spelling

. . . . . .

Students create a rainbow effect with their spelling words.

Set Up the Center

Materials

- Directions (page 23)
- Record Sheets (page 24–25)
- Alphabet stamps
- Colored pencils

1. Laminate a copy of the Directions, and copy a class set of Record Sheets. Note that two versions of the Record Sheet are provided: one for five spelling words (page 24) and one for ten spelling words (page 25). Choose the option that best meets your students' needs, which may include offering both versions at your center.

2. Display the spelling words for the week (for example, on chart paper).

3. Create and display an exemplary Record Sheet for students to use as a model.

4. Model the center work for students, repeating the procedure for several words to make sure they understand.

Extend Learning

Invite students to create additional color patterns with the spelling words on the back of their Record Sheet (or on a separate sheet of drawing paper). For example, they might alternate between two colors to create an AB pattern with the individual letters of each word or alternate among three colors to create an ABC pattern with all of the words, coloring an entire word one color.

Rainbow Spelling

Directions

1. Choose three different colored pencils.

2. Read the list of spelling words.

3. Use a colored pencil to write the first spelling word on your Record Sheet.

4. Use a different color to write the spelling word again on the line next to it.

5. Use the last pencil to write the word one more time on the third line in that row.

6. Repeat steps 3–5 for each spelling word.

Rainbow Spelling

1. _____

2. _____

3. _____

4. _____

5. _____

Name

Date

Rainbow Spelling

1. _____

2. _____

3. _____

4. _____

5. _____

6. _____

7. _____

8. _____

9. _____

10. _____

20 Super Spelling Centers
© 2012 by Erica Bohrer,
Scholastic Teaching Resources

Mix It and Fix It

This center offers a fun twist on using magnetic letters to practice spelling words. Students first arrange the magnetic letters to spell a word. Then they "mix it" and "fix it" for repeated practice.

Set Up the Center

1. Laminate a copy of the Directions, and copy a class set of Record Sheets. Note that a Record Sheet is provided for both five spelling words (page 28) and ten spelling words (page 29). Choose the option that best meets your students' needs, which may include offering both versions at your center.

2. Display the spelling words for the week (for example, on chart paper).

3. Create and display an exemplary Record Sheet for students to use as a model.

4. Model the center work for students, repeating the procedure for several words to make sure they understand.

Materials

- Directions (page 27)
- Record Sheets (pages 28–29)
- Magnetic letters (multiple sets of the alphabet)
- Shallow containers (such as baskets)
- Cookie sheets (metal/magnetic; one for each student working at the center)

Extend Learning

To extend learning, invite students to pair up and play a "Mix It and Fix It" game:

- ❋ One student secretly chooses a word from the completed Record Sheet, collects the magnetic letters to spell the word, and then places them in random order on the cookie sheet.

- ❋ The other student rearranges the letters to spell the word.

Guide students to use strategies for figuring out which word the mixed-up letters spell. For example, they can count the number of mixed-up letters, and then look at their list to find words with the same number of letters. Or they might notice, for example, that the mixed-up letters include a *p*, then find words on their Record Sheet that also have that letter.

20 Super Spelling Centers © 2012 by Erica Bohrer, Scholastic Teaching Resources

Mix It and Fix It

1. Read the list of spelling words.

2. Write the first spelling word on your Record Sheet.

3. Find the magnetic letters to spell that word. Place the letters on the cookie sheet to spell the word.

4. Mix up the magnetic letters. Write the mixed-up word on your Record Sheet.

5. Now fix the magnetic letters to spell the word again. Write the fixed word on your Record Sheet.

6. Repeat steps 2–5 to mix and fix all of your spelling words.

Record Sheet

Mix It and Fix It

Spelling Word	Mix It!	Fix It!
1.		
2.		
3.		
4.		
5.		

Name   Date

Mix It and Fix It

Spelling Word	Mix It!	Fix It!
1.		
2.		
3.		
4.		
5.		
6.		
7.		
8.		
9.		
10.		

Roll a Word

Students roll a word cube and record results on a graph to find the winning spelling word.

Set Up the Center

1. Laminate a copy of the Directions, and copy a class set of Record Sheets. Write the spelling words in the left column on the Record Sheet. Note that this Record Sheet accommodates up to six words. To use this activity with more than six words, have students complete a second Record Sheet.

2. Copy the Word Cube Pattern on cardstock and write a spelling word on each side. Cut out the cube and assemble as shown. Note that this center works with six spelling words (one for each side of the cube). If you have a list of five spelling words, you may choose to add a bonus word. If you have ten spelling words, you may want to make two cubes and repeat two spelling words or add two bonus words. Students can play the game two times, once with each cube, to practice all of their spelling words.

3. Create and display an exemplary Record Sheet for students to use as a model.

4. Model the center work for students, repeating the procedure for several words to make sure they understand. Demonstrate how to answer the questions to tell which word "won" (filled up its spaces first) and which word "lost" (filled up the fewest spaces). Explain that two or more words may "tie" for last place, and in this case, students should write all of these words.

Materials

- Directions (page 31)
- Record Sheet (page 32)
- Word Cube Pattern (page 33)

Extend Learning

Invite students to practice their words with a game of catch. Students toss the cube back and forth with a partner, calling out the word that lands faceup in their hands for the other to spell.

Roll a Word

1. Roll the word cube.

2. Read the spelling word that is face up.

3. Write the word next to the matching spelling word on your Record Sheet.

4. Repeat steps 1–3 until you have a "winning" word. This is the first word to fill all the spaces.

5. Then complete the bottom section of the Record Sheet.

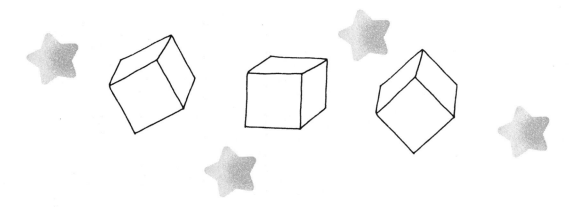

Name

Date

Roll a Word

1 Which word won? _____

2 Which word lost? If two or more words "tie" for last place, write them all.

_____

3 Write a sentence using as many of your spelling words as you can.

_____

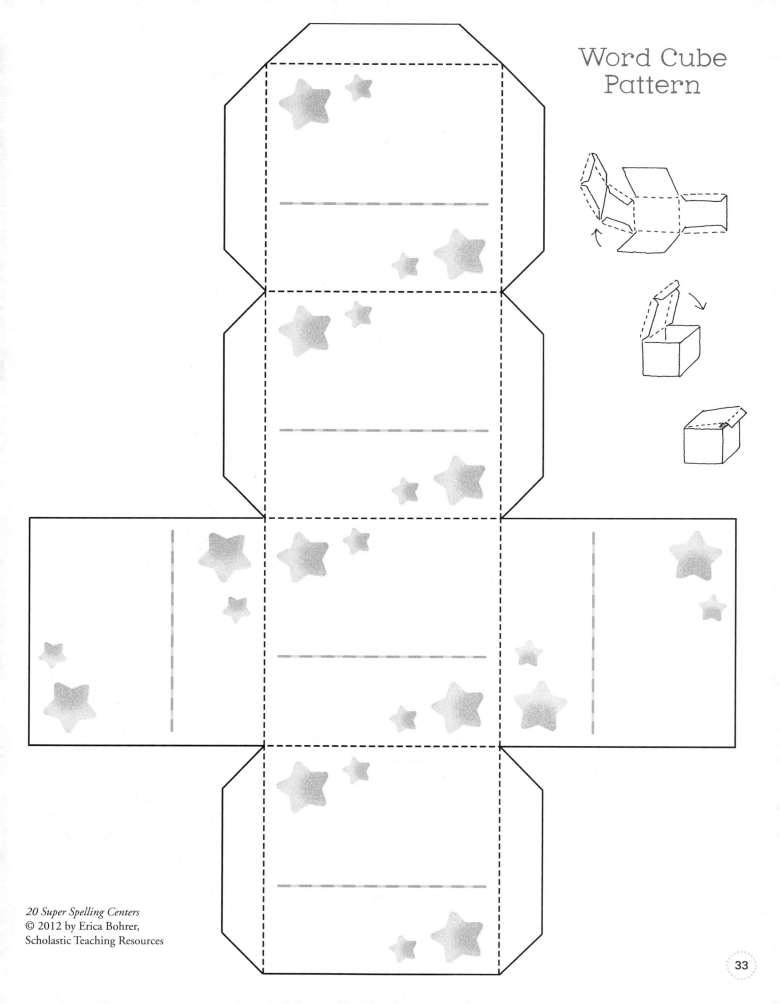

Word Cube Pattern

20 Super Spelling Centers
© 2012 by Erica Bohrer,
Scholastic Teaching Resources

33

Initial-Sound Picture Match

Students write their spelling words, then practice initial letter-sound correspondence by matching a picture to the first letter of each spelling word.

Set Up the Center

1. Laminate a copy of the Directions, and copy a class set of Record Sheets.

2. Copy a class set of the Picture Tiles. Note that this center works best when each spelling word begins with a different letter. If this is not the case with your spelling list, you will need to provide multiple copies of the Picture Tiles sheet for each student.

3. Display the spelling words for the week (for example, on chart paper).

4. Create and display an exemplary Record Sheet for students to use as a model.

5. Model the center work for students, repeating the procedure for several words to make sure students understand.

Extend Learning

Invite students to select several remaining pictures, glue them to the back of their paper, and write words that match the initial sound.

Tip

You may want to precut the pictures and organize them by initial sound in sorting trays (or egg cartons). As an alternative to the Pictures Tiles provided on page 37, students can cut out pictures from old workbooks or magazines to match the initial sound of their spelling words.

Initial-Sound Picture Match

Directions

1. Read the list of spelling words.

2. Write the first spelling word on your Record Sheet.

3. Find the picture that has the same beginning sound as that spelling word.

4. Cut out the picture. Glue it in the box next to the spelling word.

5. Repeat steps 2–4 to match a picture to each spelling word.

Initial-Sound Picture Match

1.

2.

3.

4.

5.

6.

7.

8.

9.

10.

Picture Tiles

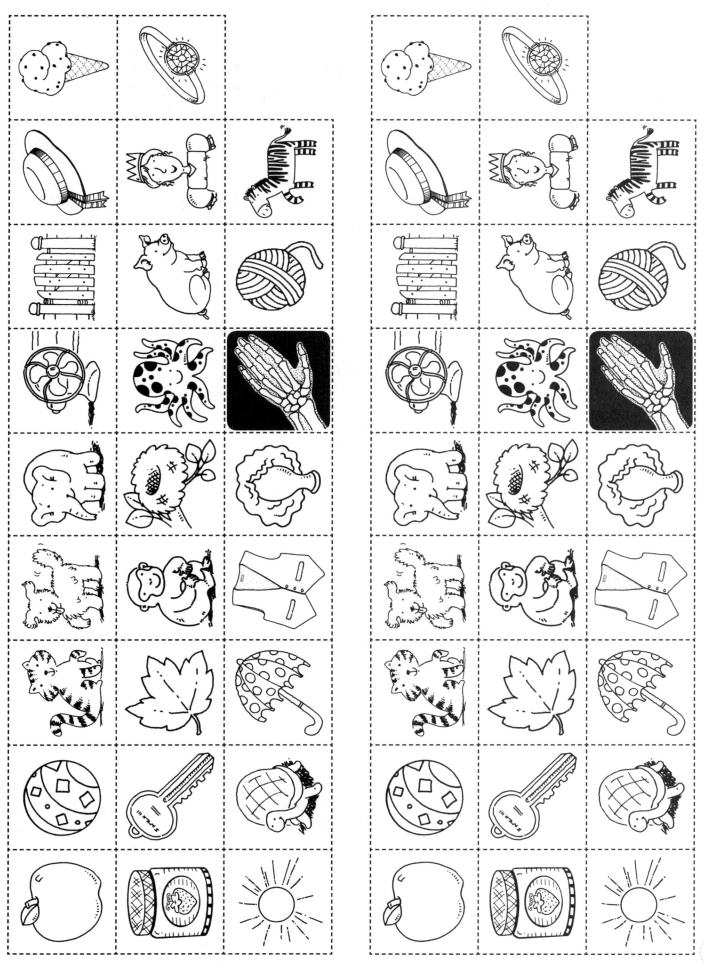

20 Super Spelling Centers © 2012 by Erica Bohrer, Scholastic Teaching Resources

Message in a Bottle

Children reveal the "message in a bottle" to practice reading and writing their spelling words.

Set Up the Center

1. Laminate a copy of the Directions, and copy a class set of Record Sheets.

2. Write each spelling word on both sides of a small strip of cardstock, then laminate. Note that the strips need to be sized to fit through the opening of the bottle.

3. Place the word cards in the plastic bottle and fill it halfway with sand. Create as many bottles as you will have students working at the center at any one time.

4. Display the spelling words for the week (for example, on chart paper).

5. Create and display an exemplary Record Sheet for students to use as a model.

6. Model the center work for students, being sure to show them how to slowly turn the bottle to reveal the words.

Materials

- Directions (page 39)
- Record Sheet (page 40)
- Liter-size plastic bottles
- Laminated word cards

Extend Learning

When students have completed the activity, they can use their words to write make-believe messages. You might provide a roll of adding-machine paper for this writing activity. Create a simple seaside display at the center and arrange students' messages inside a large "message in a bottle" cutout.

20 Super Spelling Centers © 2012 by Erica Bohrer, Scholastic Teaching Resources

Message in a Bottle

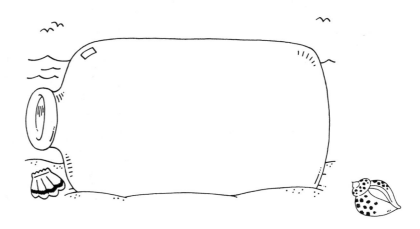

1. Slowly turn the bottle until you see a spelling word.

2. Write the spelling word on your Record Sheet.

3. Repeat steps 1 and 2 until you find and write all of your spelling words.

Name

Date

Message in a Bottle

1. _____

2. _____

3. _____

4. _____

5. _____

6. _____

7. _____

8. _____

9. _____

10. _____

20 Super Spelling Centers © 2012 by Erica Bohrer, Scholastic Teaching Resources

Text a Word

Students use cell-phone manipulatives to practice reading and writing their spelling words.

Set Up the Center

1. Laminate a copy of the Directions, and copy a class set of Record Sheets. Note that this Record Sheet accommodates up to five words. To use this activity with more than five words, have students complete a second Record Sheet.

2. Make multiple copies of the Cell Phone Patterns on cardstock. Laminate the pages, then cut apart the phones.

3. Display the spelling words for the week (for example, on chart paper).

4. Create and display an exemplary Record Sheet for students to use as a model.

5. Model the center work for students, demonstrating how to write the numbers that correspond with each letter on the keypad. For example, "air" would be "1-3-6." Make sure students understand that several letters correspond to each number.

Materials

- Directions (page 42)
- Record Sheet (page 43)
- Cell Phone Patterns (page 44)

Extend Learning

When students have completed the activity, invite them to quiz each other on the text codes. Students can take turns reading a code and figuring out the word based on the code. Remind students that several letters match each number, so there may be some "detective" work involved in figuring out the words. Students can also use their spelling words to "text" a message. Enlarge a cell phone pattern for this extension and have students write their message inside the "screen" area.

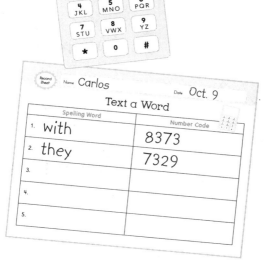

Text a Word

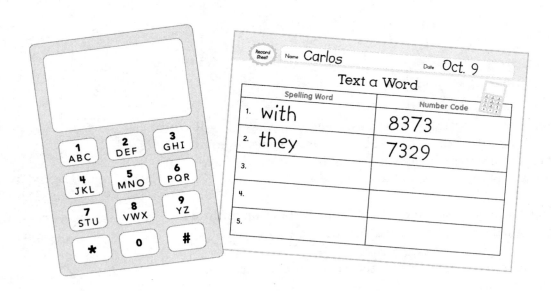

Name Carlos   Date Oct. 9

Text a Word

Spelling Word	Number Code
1. with	8373
2. they	7329
3.	
4.	
5.	

Phone keypad:
1 ABC | 2 DEF | 3 GHI
4 JKL | 5 MNO | 6 PQR
7 STU | 8 VWX | 9 YZ
* | 0 | #

Directions

1. Read the list of spelling words.

2. Write the first spelling word on your Record Sheet.

3. Then record the number code.

4. Repeat steps 2 and 3 with each spelling word.

20 Super Spelling Centers © 2012 by Erica Bohrer, Scholastic Teaching Resources

Name

Date

Text a Word

Spelling Word	Number Code
1.	
2.	
3.	
4.	
5.	

Cell Phone Patterns

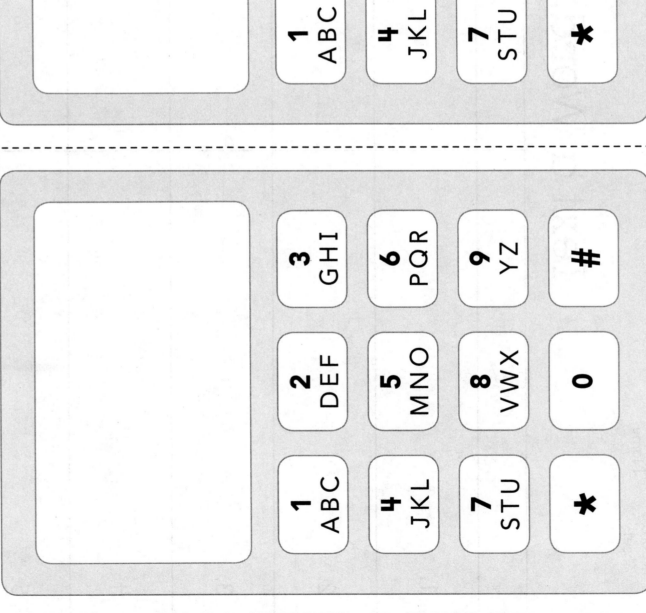

Scrapbook Spelling

Students create a scrapbook effect with their spelling words, using letters cut from magazines.

Set Up the Center

1. Precut letters from magazines. This is a good project for students to help with when they have a little extra time before school starts. Place the letters in a shallow basket or container.

2. Laminate a copy of the Directions, and copy a class set of Record Sheets. Note that this Record Sheet accommodates up to five words. To use this activity with more than five words, have students complete a second Record Sheet.

3. Display the spelling words for the week (for example, on chart paper).

4. Create and display an exemplary Record Sheet for students to use as a model. Students can also use construction paper to create their own Record Sheet, if they would like a little extra room.

5. Model the center work for students. Remind students to put the glue on the back of the letter, then place the letter on their Record Sheet.

Materials

- Directions (page 46)
- Record Sheet (page 47)
- Old magazines
- Shallow basket or container
- Construction paper (optional)
- Glue sticks

Extend Learning

When students have completed the activity, invite them to quiz each other. They can take turns covering one letter in a word and guessing the missing letter. Note that this extension does not lend itself to word-family spelling lists (such as words that all end with -at).

Scrapbook Spelling

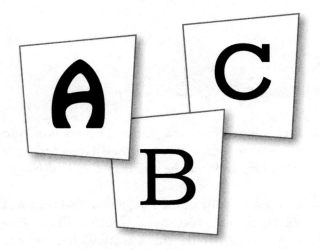

Directions

1. Read the list of spelling words.

2. Find the letters you need to spell the first word. Arrange the letters in order on the table.

3. Glue each letter in order on the Record Sheet to spell the word.

4. Repeat steps 2 and 3 to spell all of your words.

Name _____   Date _____

ScRapbook
Spelling

1. _____

2. _____

3. _____

4. _____

5. _____

Read and Write the Room

Students "read around the classroom" to find words that begin with the same letter as their spelling words.

Set Up the Center

1. Laminate a copy of the Directions, and copy a class set of Record Sheets.

2. Display the spelling words for the week (for example, on chart paper).

3. Create and display an exemplary Record Sheet for students to use as a model.

4. Provide clipboards students can use (for their Record Sheets) as they read and write words from around the room.

5. Model the center work for students, showing them how to read a spelling word, then look for a word around the room that begins with the same letter. As you model, point out that you are walking quietly around the room so that you don't disturb others.

Materials

- Directions (page 49)
- Record Sheet (page 50)
- Clipboards

Extend Learning

Students can repeat the activity to focus on other features of the same spelling words. Choose a feature that works best with your spelling words—for example, vowel sounds, consonant digraphs (such as *sh* and *th*), or number of syllables.

Read and Write the Room

Directions

1. Read the list of spelling words.

2. Write the first word on your Record Sheet.

3. Read around the room. Look for a word that begins with the same letter as the spelling word.

4. Write the word on your Record Sheet next to the spelling word.

5. Repeat steps 2–4 for all of your spelling words.

Read and Write the Room

Spelling Words	Words I Found
1.	
2.	
3.	
4.	
5.	
6.	
7.	
8.	
9.	
10.	

20 Super Spelling Centers © 2012 by Lisa Blau, Scholastic Teaching Resources

Shape Spelling

Students record their spelling words on a grid, then shade the unused boxes to make the word shapes stand out.

Set Up the Center

Materials

- Directions (page 52)
- Record Sheet (page 53)
- Crayons and colored pencils

1. Laminate a copy of the Directions, and copy a class set of Record Sheets. Note that the Record Sheets accommodate six spelling words, up to seven letters each. To use this activity with more than six words, have students complete a second Record Sheet. If your spelling list consists of longer words (more than seven letters each), use the Record Sheet as a model to create one that has more than seven spaces across.

2. Display the spelling words for the week (for example, on chart paper).

3. Create and display an exemplary Record Sheet for students to use as a model.

4. Demonstrate writing a spelling word on the grid, using one box for "short" letters (such as *c* and *o*) and two boxes for ascending and descending letters (such as *t* and *g*). Point out that you start writing your word in the center row. (This will avoid confusion for students when writing words with ascenders and descenders.) Show students that you color carefully around the boxes that have letters. (See samples, right.)

Extend Learning

Enlarge the grid paper, then color in the boxes to represent the shape of each spelling word, coloring one box for "short" letters (such as *c* and *o*) and two boxes for ascending and descending letters (such as *t* and *g*). For example, for the word *big*, you would color one box for the letter *i*, then two boxes one on top of the other for each of the letters *b* and *g*. Cut out the filled-in boxes for each word (the shape) and glue them to index cards. Write each matching spelling word on the back. Have students look at the shape and guess the word, then look on the back to check their answer. Remind students that they should use the spelling list for hints.

Shape Spelling

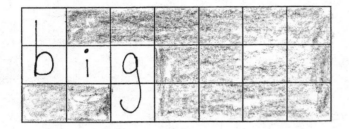

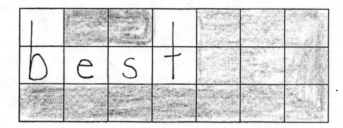

1. Read the list of spelling words.

2. Write the first spelling word on your Record Sheet.

3. Color the boxes around the letters of your spelling word. You can use one color or more than one color.

4. Repeat steps 2 and 3 for all of your spelling words.

20 Super Spelling Centers © 2012 by Erica Bohrer, Scholastic Teaching Resources

Name

Date

Shape Spelling

1

2

3

4

5

6

20 Super Spelling Centers © 2012 by Erica Bohrer, Scholastic Teaching Resources

Spelling Soup

· · · · · ·

Students serve up some alphabet soup to practice their spelling words.

Set Up the Center

1. Laminate a copy of the Directions, and copy a class set of Record Sheets. Note that this Record Sheet accommodates up to seven words. To use this activity with more than seven words, have students complete a second Record Sheet.

2. Place letter tiles inside a large pot. A variation would be to write letters on smooth pasta such as penne, and place those in the pot.

3. Provide a small plastic bowl for each student working at the center, and a ladle for them to share.

4. Display the spelling words for the week (for example, on chart paper).

5. Create and display an exemplary Record Sheet for students to use as a model.

6. Model the center work for students, making sure to demonstrate with a volunteer how to take turns scooping out letters. Remind students to ladle out more letters if they do not have the ones they need to make their spelling word.

Materials

- Directions (page 55)
- Record Sheet (page 56)
- Letter tiles (multiple sets)
- Large pot
- Ladle
- Plastic bowls

Extend Learning

When students have completed the activity, invite them to mix up the letter tiles for each word and then put them in order again.

Spelling Soup

Directions

1. Read the list of spelling words.

2. Use the ladle to scoop out letters from the pot. Pour them into your bowl.

3. Look at the letters. Try to make one of your spelling words out of the letters. Scoop out more letters if you don't have the letters you need.

4. Write the spelling word you make on your Record Sheet.

5. Repeat steps 2–4 until you have made all of your spelling words.

20 Super Spelling Centers © 2012 by Erica Bohrer, Scholastic Teaching Resources

Name

Date

Spelling Soup

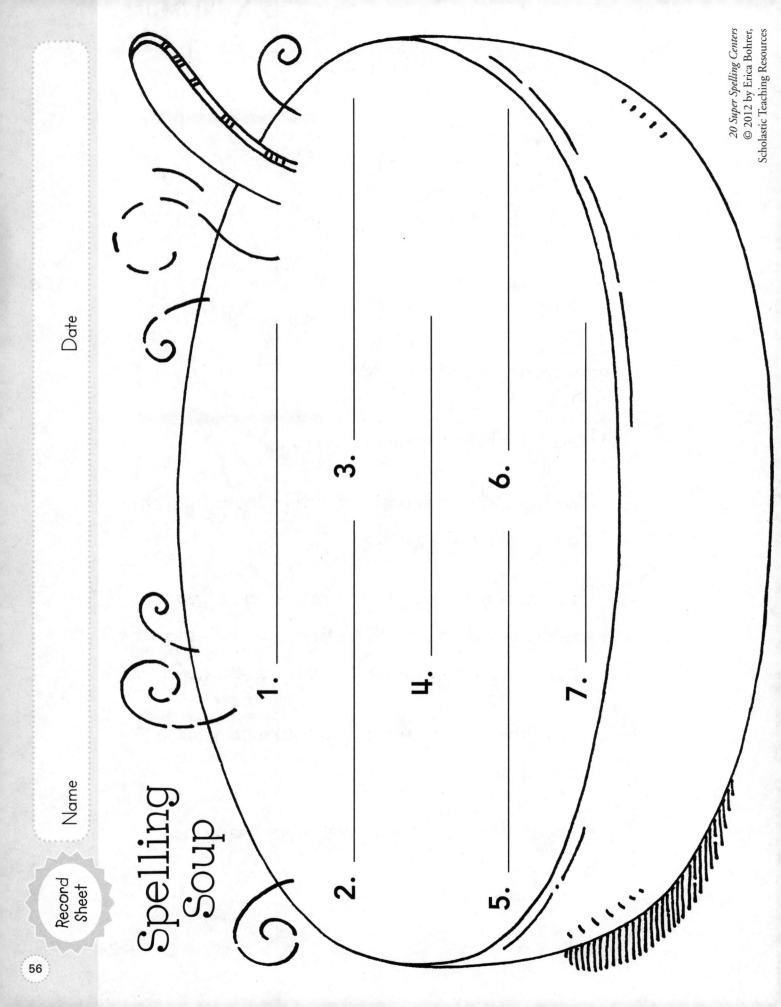

1.

2.

3.

4.

5.

6.

7.

20 Super Spelling Centers
© 2012 by Erica Bohrer,
Scholastic Teaching Resources

Sail Away With Vowels and Consonants

Students focus on individual letters of their spelling words with this sailboat-themed activity.

Set Up the Center

1. Laminate a copy of the Directions, and copy a class set of Record Sheets. Copy, color, and laminate several copies of the Sailboat Work Mat. Note that this Record Sheet accommodates up to five words. To use this activity with more than five words, have students complete a second Record Sheet.

2. Display the spelling words for the week (for example, on chart paper).

3. Create and display an exemplary Record Sheet for students to use as a model.

4. Model the center work for students, making sure to review vowels and consonants as you sort them onto the mat. (You might display a vowel and consonant chart for reference.)

Materials

- Directions (page 58)
- Sailboat Work Mat (page 59)
- Record Sheet (page 60)
- Letter tiles

Extend Learning

When students have completed the activity, invite them to pair up and play a vowel and consonant game:

- One student secretly chooses a word from the completed Record Sheet, collects the letter tiles needed to spell that word, and sorts them by vowels and consonants on the Sailboat Work Mat.

- The other student arranges the letters to spell the word.

- Students trade places and play again with a new word.

Guide students to use strategies for figuring out which word the vowels and consonants spell. For example, they can count the total number of letters, and then look at their list to find words with the same number of letters. Or they might notice, for example, that one of the consonants is a *b*, then find words on their Record Sheet that also have that letter.

Sail Away With Vowels and Consonants

Directions

1. Read the list of spelling words.

2. Find the letters to spell the first word. Place them on the Sailboat Work Mat.

3. Sort the vowels and consonants on the sails of the sailboat.

4. Write the spelling word, the vowels, and the consonants on your Record Sheet.

5. Repeat steps 2–4 for all of your spelling words.

20 Super Spelling Centers © 2012 by Erica Bohrer, Scholastic Teaching Resources

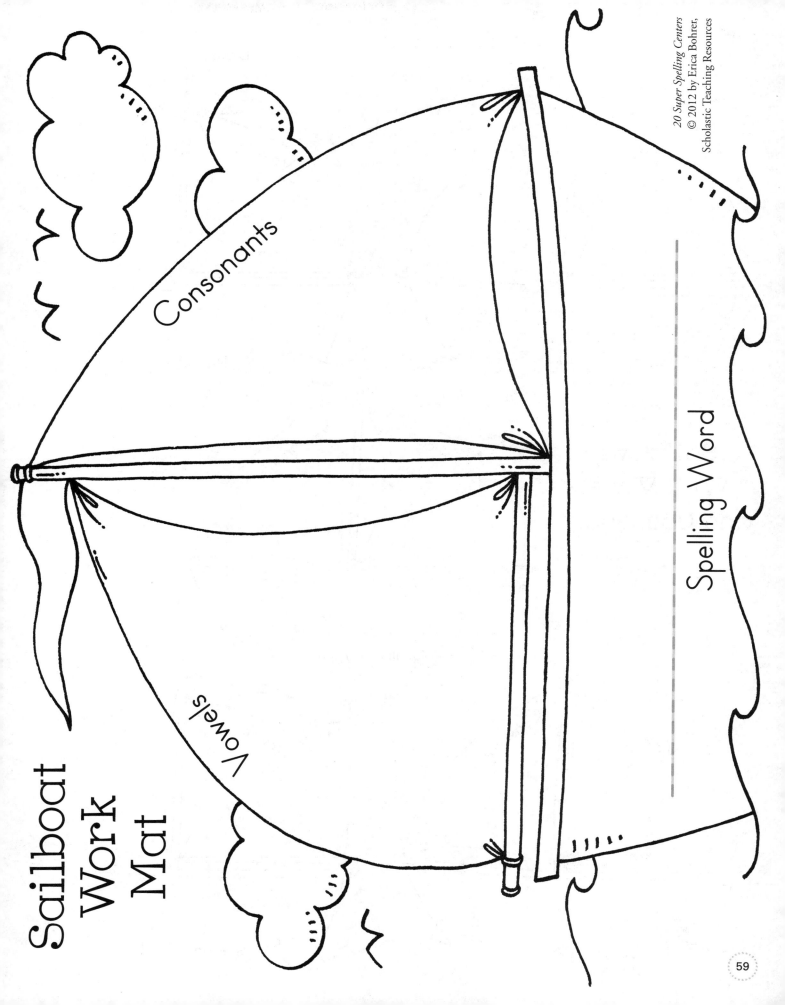

Sailboat Work Mat

Consonants

Vowels

Spelling Word

20 Super Spelling Centers
© 2012 by Erica Bohrer,
Scholastic Teaching Resources

Record Sheet

Name Date

1

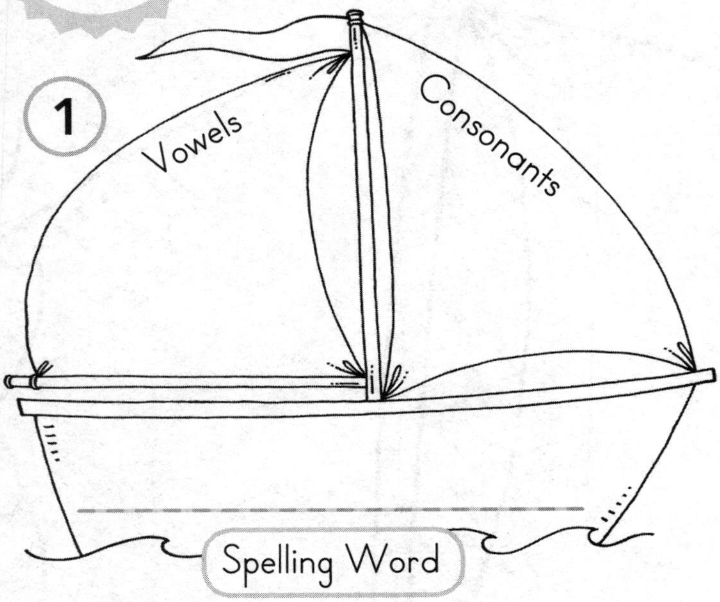
Vowels
Consonants
Spelling Word

2

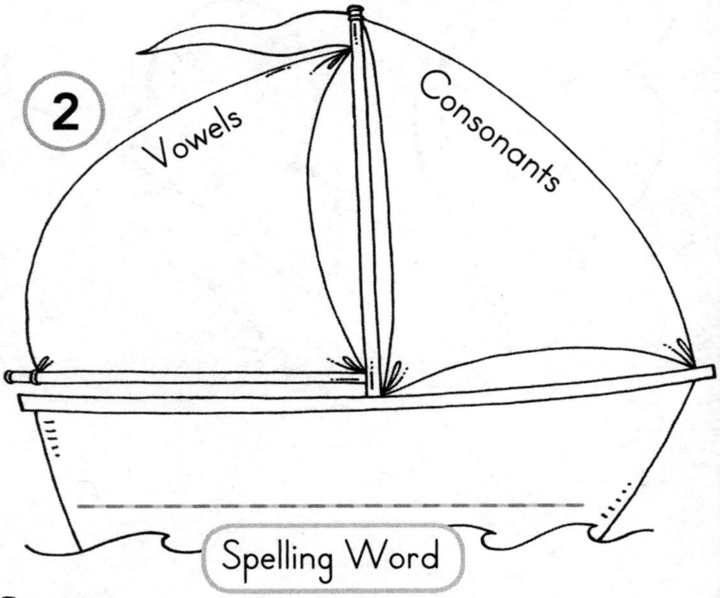
Vowels
Consonants
Spelling Word

Sail Away With Vowels and Consonants

3

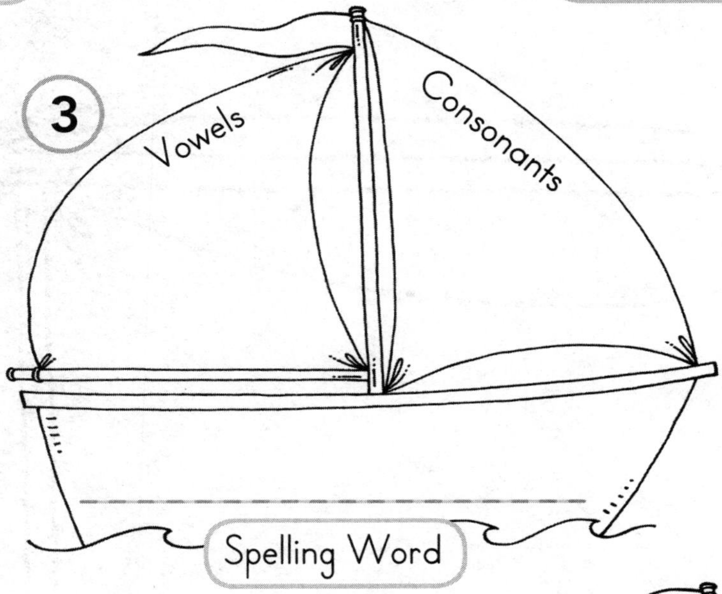
Vowels
Consonants
Spelling Word

4

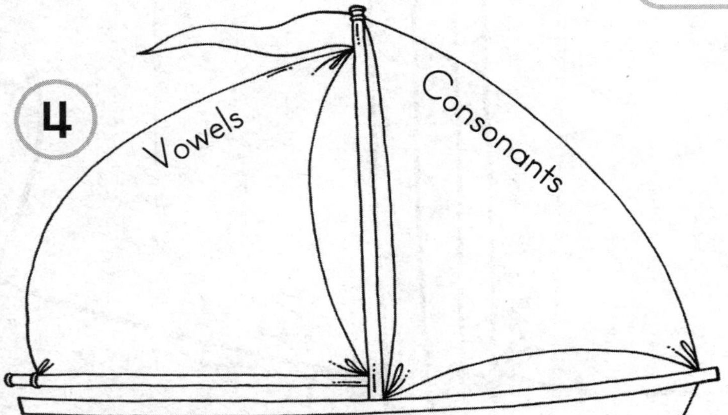
Vowels
Consonants
Spelling Word

5

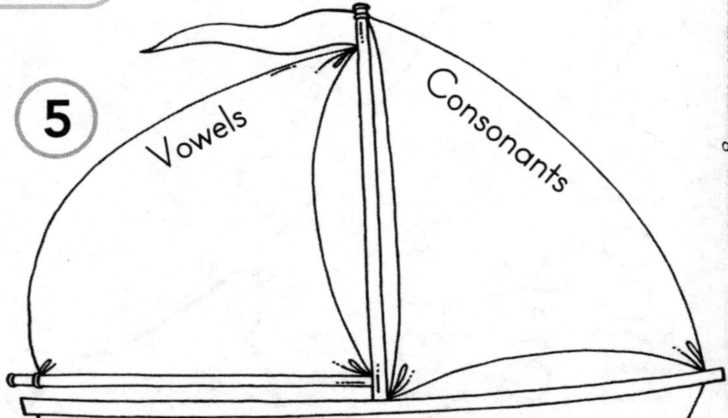
Vowels
Consonants
Spelling Word

Word Hunt

A scavenger hunt encourages students to focus on particular features of each of their spelling words.

Set Up the Center

Materials

♦ Directions (page 62)
♦ Record Sheets (pages 63–64)

1. Laminate a copy of the Directions, and copy a class set of Record Sheets. Note that you will need to complete the blanks on the Record Sheet to go with your specific spelling words. Also, a Record Sheet is provided for both five spelling words (page 63) and ten spelling words (page 64). Choose the option that best meets your students' needs, which may include offering both versions at your center.

2. Display the spelling words for the week (for example, on chart paper).

3. Create and display an exemplary Record Sheet for students to use as a model.

4. Model the center work for students.

Extend Learning

When students have completed the activity, invite them to create their own word hunts to share with classmates.

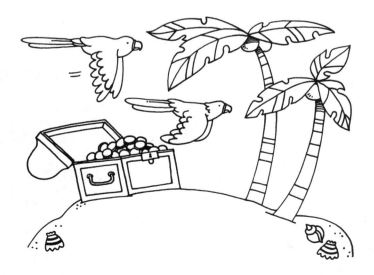

Word Hunt

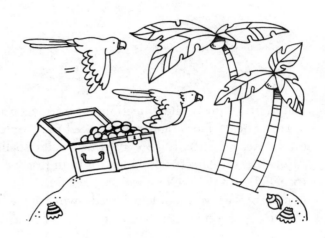

> **Directions**

1. Read the list of spelling words.

2. Read the first Word Hunt clue.

3. Find the spelling word that matches the clue. Write it on your Record Sheet.

4. Repeat steps 2 and 3 to complete the Record Sheet.

20 Super Spelling Centers © 2012 by Erica Bohrer, Scholastic Teaching Resources

Name _____

Date _____

Word Hunt

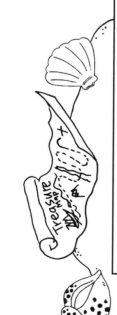

Clue	Spelling Word
1. A word that begins with ___	
2. A word that rhymes with ___	
3. A word with ___ as the second letter	
4. A word that is ___ letters long	
5. A word that ends with ___	

20 Super Spelling Centers © 2012 by Erica Bohrer, Scholastic Teaching Resources

Name _____   Date _____

Word Hunt

Clue	Spelling Word
1. A word that begins with _____	
2. A word with _____ vowels	
3. A word with _____ consonants	
4. A word that is _____ letters long	
5. A word that ends with _____	
6. A word with _____ as the third letter	
7. A word that contains _____	
8. A word with a _____ and a _____	
9. A word that rhymes with _____	
10. The word that you have not used yet	

20 Super Spelling Centers © 2012 by Erica Bohrer, Scholastic Teaching Resources

Laundry Letters

Students hang laundry out to dry to fill in the missing letters of their spelling words.

Materials

- Directions (page 66)
- Record Sheet (page 67)
- Laundry Patterns (page 68)
- Shallow containers (such as baskets)
- Clothespins
- Clotheslines (yarn or thin rope)

Set Up the Center

1. Laminate a copy of the Directions, and copy a class set of Record Sheets. Cut each Record Sheet in half as indicated and tape together to create a horizontal laundry line effect.

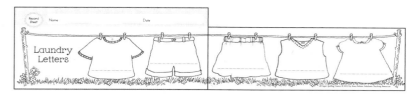

2. Copy and cut apart the Laundry Patterns. Write a spelling word on each piece of laundry, making sure to leave out the first letter of the spelling word. Color the laundry and place in a shallow container. Make as many sets of laundry as students who may be working at the center at any one time.

3. Write the missing letters on clothespins. (Repeat for each set of laundry.) Place the clothespins in a shallow container with the clotheslines.

4. Display the spelling words for the week (for example, on chart paper).

5. Create and display an exemplary Record Sheet for students to use as a model.

6. Model the center work for students. Be sure to show them that you place the yarn on the table to create a "clothesline." Demonstrate how to clip the clothing pattern to the clothesline to complete the word.

Extend Learning

When students have completed the activity, invite them to use their Record Sheets to quiz each other. Students can take turns reading the letters in a word (saying "blank" for the missing letter) and telling both the missing letter and the word.

Laundry Letters

street

Directions

1. Read the list of spelling words.

2. Take a piece of laundry.

3. Look at the letters on the laundry.
   Think about the missing first letter.

4. Find the clothespin with the missing letter.

5. Use the clothespin to hang the laundry on the line.

6. Write the word on your Record Sheet.

7. Repeat steps 2–6 to hang all of your spelling words on the clothesline.

20 Super Spelling Centers © 2012 by Erica Bohrer, Scholastic Teaching Resources

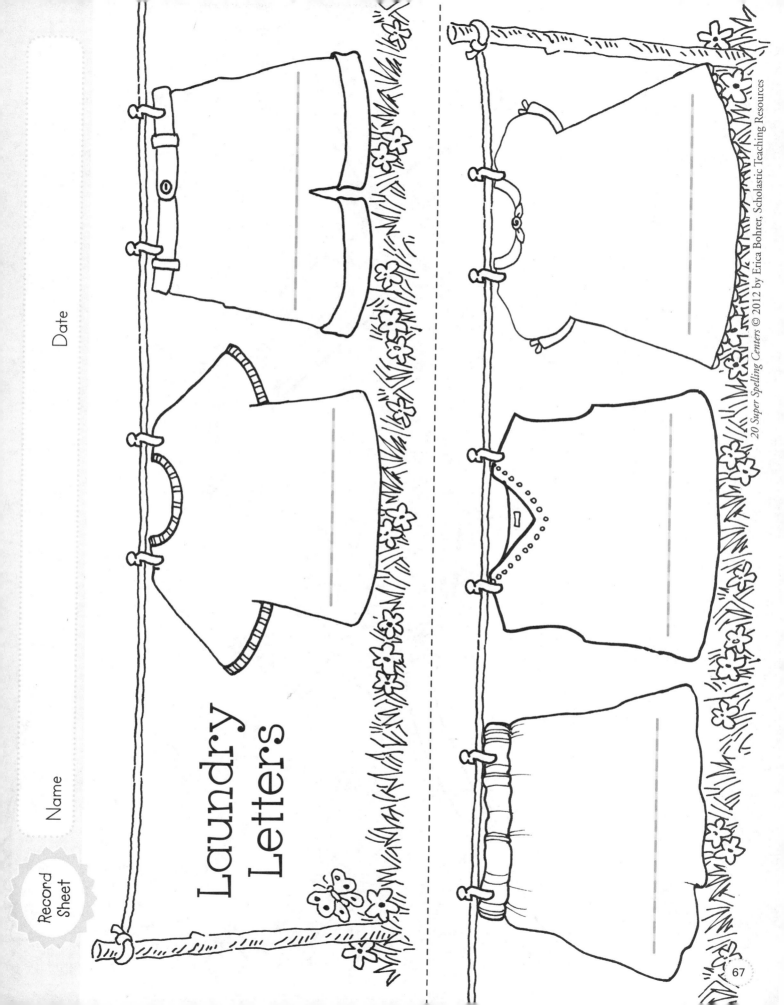

Name

Date

Laundry
Letters

20 Super Spelling Centers © 2012 by Erica Bohrer, Scholastic Teaching Resources

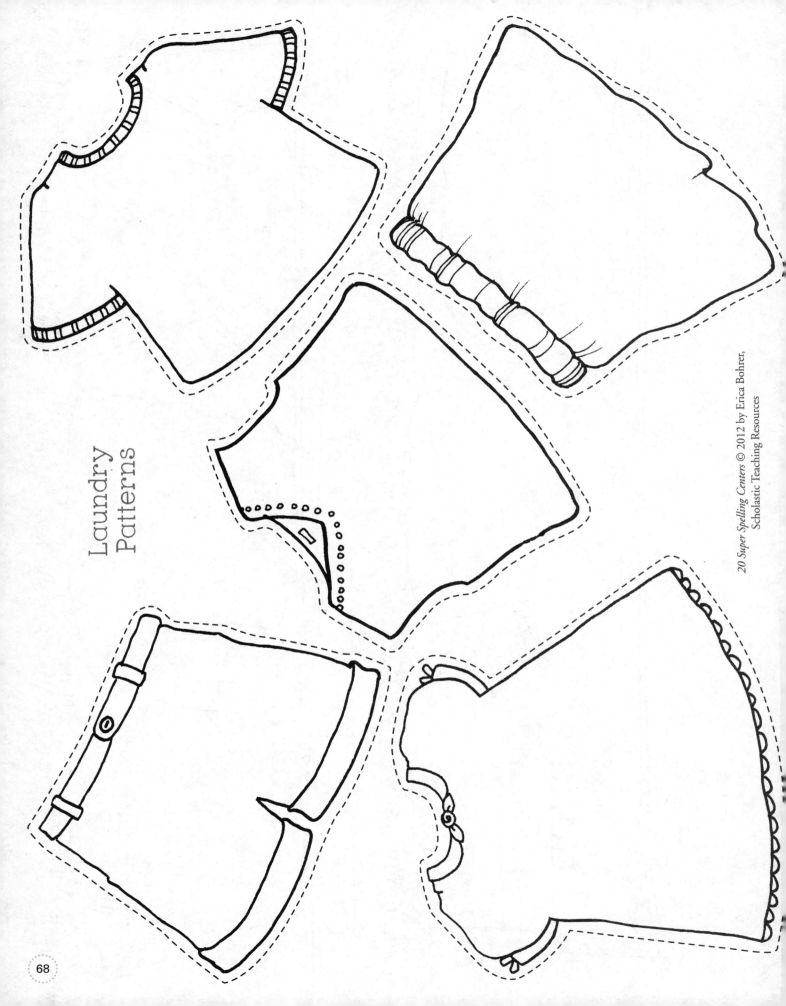

Laundry Patterns

On Your Mark, Get Set, Spell!

With this simple board game, students quiz each other on their spelling words as they race to the finish line.

Set Up the Center

1. Laminate a copy of the Directions, and copy a class set of Record Sheets. Note that this Record Sheet accommodates up to eight words. To use this activity with more than eight words, have students complete a second Record Sheet.

2. Copy, color, and laminate the Racetrack Game Board.

3. Create word cards by writing the spelling words on index cards.

4. Place a number cube and game markers, such as small toy cars, at the center.

5. Create and display an exemplary Record Sheet for students to use as a model.

6. Model the center work for students. Remind students to record each spelling word as they are quizzed. Students can play with partners.

Materials

- Directions (page 70)
- Record Sheet (page 71)
- Racetrack Game Board (page 72)
- Two pennies
- Small toy cars (or other game markers)
- Index cards

Extend Learning

When students have completed the activity, they can use the word cards to quiz each other. Working with a partner, students can each take half of the cards and take turns reading words for the other to spell. Consider making an extra set of center materials (in a large resealable bag) for students to take home and play with their family.

On Your Mark, Get Set, Spell!

Directions (for two players)

1. Each player takes a game marker and places it on Start.

2. One player takes a word card and reads the word.

3. The other player spells the word.

4. If the player spells the word correctly, he or she "tosses" the pennies and moves as follows:

   - both heads: 3 spaces
   - both tails: 2 spaces
   - one heads, one tails: 1 space

5. Both players write the word on their Record Sheet.

6. Players take turns reading and spelling words. The first player to get to the finish line wins.

20 Super Spelling Centers © 2012 by Erica Bohrer, Scholastic Teaching Resources

Name _____   Date _____

On Your Mark, Get Set, Spell!

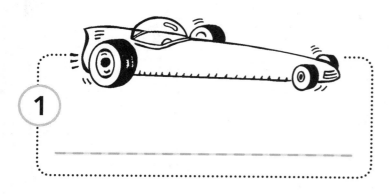

1 _____

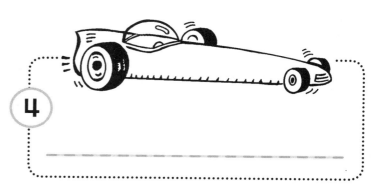

2 _____

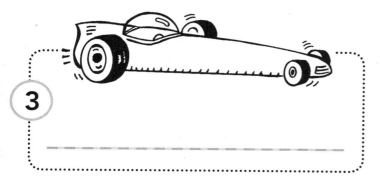

3 _____

4 _____

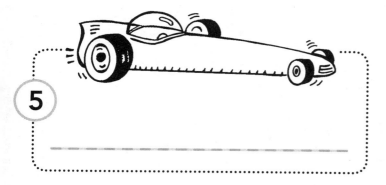

5 _____

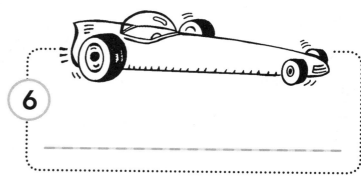

6 _____

7 _____

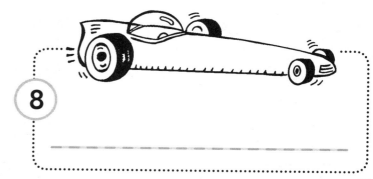

8 _____

Racetrack Game Board

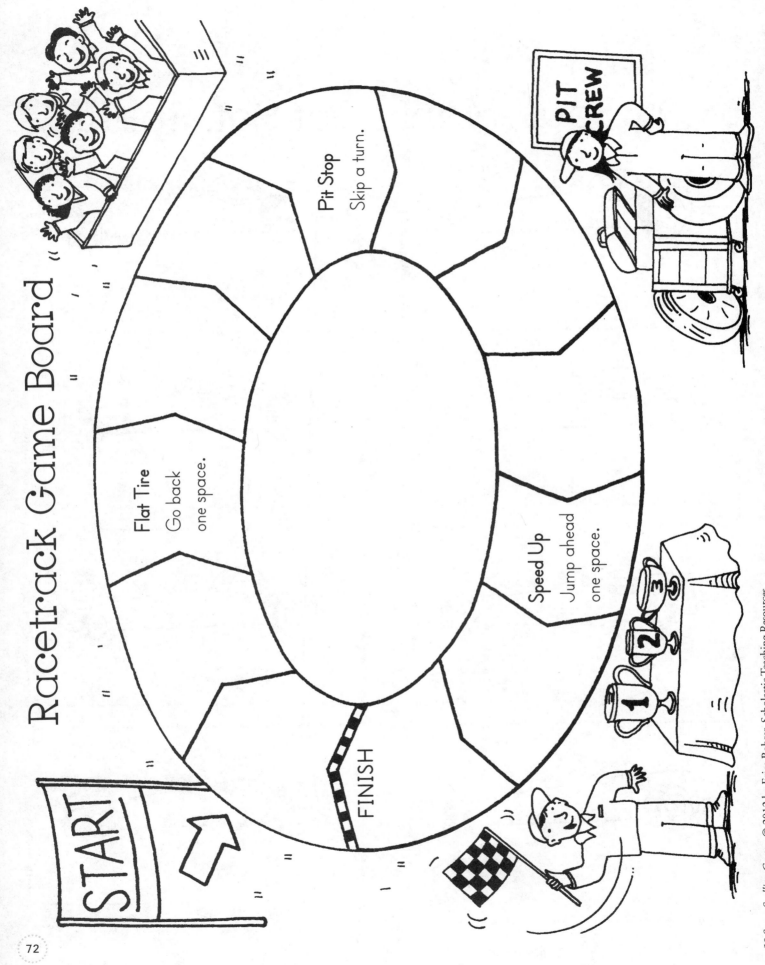

START

Flat Tire
Go back one space.

Pit Stop
Skip a turn.

PIT CREW

Speed Up
Jump ahead one space.

FINISH

ABC Order Train

Students arrange train cars that are "carrying" their spelling words in alphabetical order.

Set Up the Center

1. Laminate a copy of the Directions, and copy a class set of Record Sheets. Note that this Record Sheet accommodates up to eight spelling words. To use this activity with more than eight words, you can add on to the "train tracks," renumbering to match.

2. Copy, color, and cut apart the train cars. Make as many train cars as words on your spelling list. Write a spelling word on each train car, then place in a shallow container.

3. Create and display an exemplary Record Sheet for students to use as a model.

4. Model the center work for students, making sure to review the concept of alphabetical order. Remind students to work together at this center and to refer to an alphabet chart or alphabet strip when needed.

Materials

- Directions (page 74)
- Train Car Patterns (page 75)
- Record Sheet (page 76)
- Shallow containers (such as baskets)
- Alphabet chart or alphabet strip

Extend Learning

When students have completed the activity, invite them to mix up the train cars. Students can take turns with a partner placing the train cars back in alphabetical order.

ABC Order Train

ABC Order Train

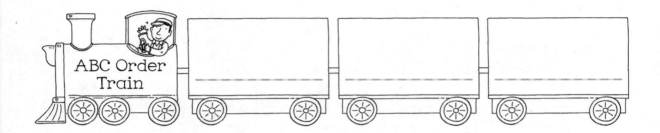

ABC Order Train

Directions

1. Place the train engine on the table.

2. Take a train car. Read the word.

3. Place the train car behind the train engine.

4. Repeat steps 2 and 3 until all the train cars are in ABC order.

5. Write the words in ABC order on your Record Sheet.

20 Super Spelling Centers © 2012 by Erica Bohrer, Scholastic Teaching Resources

ABC Order Train

Name   Date

ABC Order Train

1.

2.

3.

4.

5.

6.

7.

8.

Spelling Bees

Students fill in the missing letters in their spelling words.

Set Up the Center

1. Laminate a copy of the Directions, and copy a class set of Record Sheets.

2. Write a spelling word three times across a sentence strip. Omit a different letter of the word each time—for example, for the word *tree*, you might write _ree, t_ee, and tr_e. (See sample, right.) Leave a blank space (sized to fit a Bee Pattern) for each omitted letter. Repeat for each spelling word. As a variation, you can omit more than one adjoining letter in each word to focus on a spelling pattern, such as a digraph or vowel pair. In this case, write the missing letters on one bee.

3. Copy, color, and cut apart the Bee Patterns. Write each omitted letter on a bee.

4. Place each sentence strip and set of bees in an envelope. Write the word on the front.

5. Display the spelling words for the week (for example, on chart paper).

6. Create and display an exemplary Record Sheet for students to use as a model.

7. Model the center work for students, repeating the procedure for several words to make sure they understand.

Materials

- Directions (page 78)
- Record Sheet (page 79)
- Bee Patterns (page 80)
- Sentence strips
- Envelopes

Extend Learning

When students have completed the activity, they can write the spelling words on the back of their Record Sheet and omit letters. Have them take turns with a partner guessing each other's missing letters.

Spelling Bees

Directions

1. Read the list of spelling words.

2. Choose an envelope.
   Take out the sentence strip and bees.

3. Arrange the bees to fill in the missing letters.

4. Write the spelling word on your Record Sheet.

5. Return the sentence strip and bees
   to the envelope.

6. Repeat steps 2–5 with each envelope
   to complete your Record Sheet.

20 Super Spelling Centers © 2012 by Erica Bohrer, Scholastic Teaching Resources

Name _____

Date _____

Record Sheet

1. _____

2. _____

3. _____

4. _____

5. _____

6. _____

7. _____

8. _____

9. _____

10. _____

Spelling Bees

20 Super Spelling Centers © 2012 by Erica Bohrer, Scholastic Teaching Resources

Bee Patterns

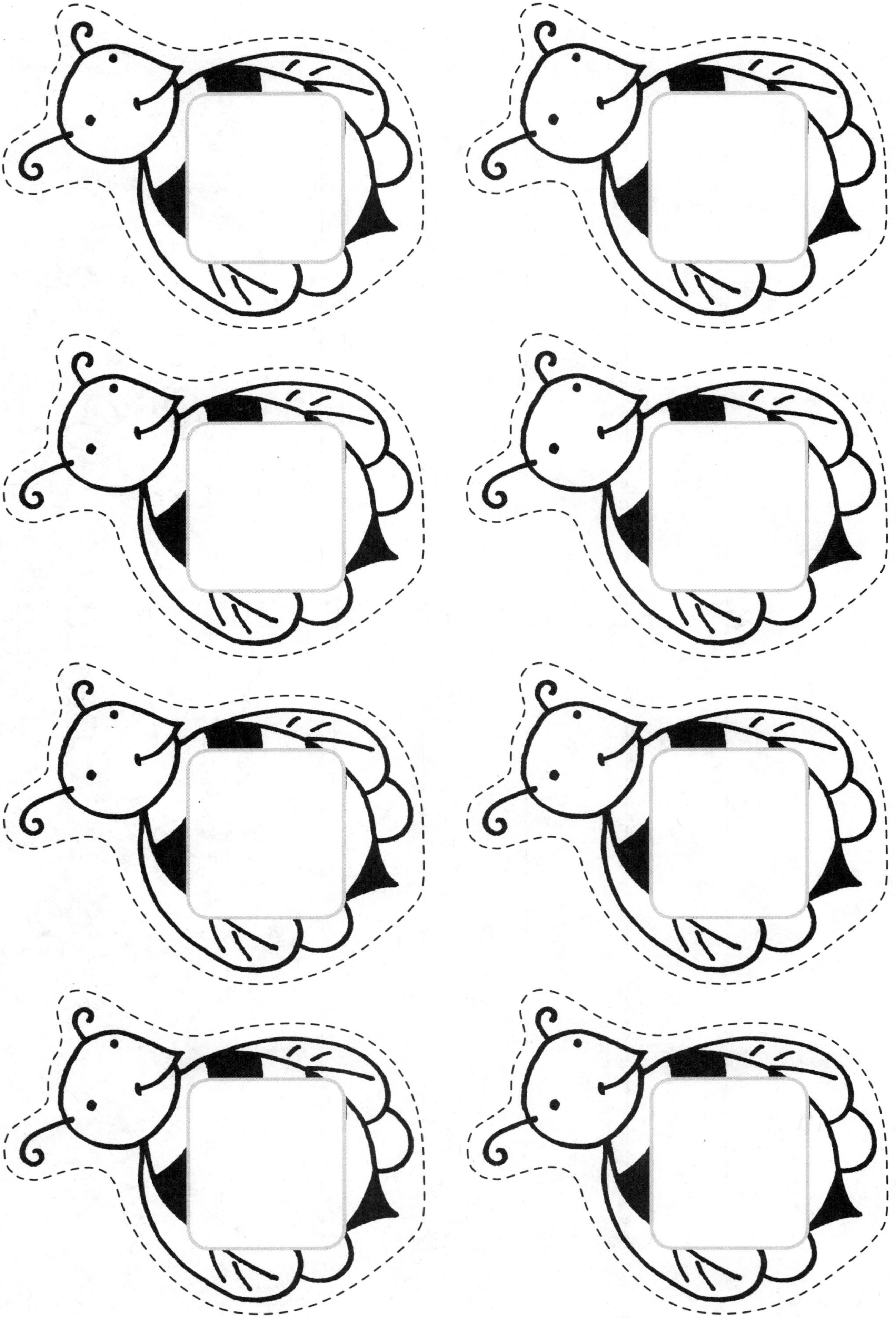